HER FEARLESS RUN

KATHRINE SWITZER'S HISTORIC BOSTON MARATHON

KIM CHAFFEE   ILLUSTRATED BY ELLEN ROONEY

PAGE
STREET
KIDS

PAT, PAT, PAT

The summer sun beat down on twelve-year-old Kathrine. She held out her piece of chalk and marked the tree as she ran past again. Two laps to go. Kathrine dripped with sweat. Her legs felt like noodles, but she kept running.

One lap to go . . . just a few more feet . . . a few steps . . .

1 MILE!

Kathrine held her head high and tried to catch her breath. But . . .

The mailman stared. The milkman asked if she was okay. Because in 1959, it was strange to see a girl running.

Girls weren't supposed to sweat. Girls weren't supposed to compete. They were too weak, too fragile, for sports. That's what most people thought.

But not Kathrine.

She thought running was magic.

PAT, PAT, PAT, PAT

At seventeen, Kathrine traded laps in her back yard for laps at the Lynchburg College track, where she was a student.

3 MILES . . .

One rainy afternoon, Kathrine noticed the men's running coach waiting for her along the track.

"Can you run a mile?" he asked.

"I can run three," Kathrine scoffed.

Although there was no women's running team, Lynchburg was one of the few schools that allowed women to run in men's races. The team needed more runners, and Kathrine was eager to join.

Lynchburg Runners
Take on Boston
by K.V. Switzer

PAT, PAT, PAT, PAT, PAT

Four laps around . . . three laps to go . . . two laps . . . one more . . . She finished her first competitive mile!

One day, Kathrine interviewed two teammates for the sports section of the school newspaper. They had just run the Boston Marathon, a race that was more than twenty-six miles long! Kathrine's eyes shined.

She had never heard of anyone running that far.

Kathrine began classes at Syracuse University later that fall.

Like Lynchburg, there was no women's running team. Syracuse didn't allow women to compete in races, but the men's running coach invited Kathrine to practice with them.

Arnie Briggs, the volunteer team manager, beamed. "I've been here twenty years, and we've never had a girl before!"

Kathrine felt welcome.

PAT, PAT, PAT, PAT, PAT, PAT

At first, the others ran just ahead of Kathrine, and she struggled to keep up. Soon there was no one in sight. So Arnie started running with her. Day after day, month after month, they ran side by side.

5 MILES . . . 10 MILES . . .

Arnie told lots of stories to pass the time. Most of them were about the Boston Marathon. He had run it fifteen times. One winter's day, Kathrine confessed to Arnie that she wanted to run it too.

"Women can't do that kind of distance," he replied. "They can't run that long."

"But I run six or even ten miles with you every night!" Kathrine shot back.

Arnie always told her how good she was at running. How could he doubt her? Kathrine knew that ten miles was a long way from twenty-six. But she believed she could run any distance if she trained for it. And she wanted to train for the Boston Marathon.

"If any woman can run a marathon, I believe you could," Arnie admitted. "But even you would have to prove it to me."

"You're on!" replied Kathrine.

PAT, PAT, PAT, PAT, PAT, PAT, PAT

Kathrine ran through the bitter cold of January and February and March.

12 MILES . . . 14 MILES . . .

Snowbanks piled high. Sidewalks disappeared. It was hard to run on the roads safely. Her legs ached, and blisters covered her feet.

16 MILES . . . 18 MILES . . .

She cut triangle wedges out of her sneakers just to get them over her swollen toes. On her last training run, Kathrine ran . . . and ran . . . and ran . . .

31 MILES!

That was almost five miles farther than the marathon.
Kathrine was ready.

But Kathrine had a problem. For seventy years, only men had been allowed to wear an official race number while running the Boston Marathon. Would she be accepted as a woman? Should she run without signing up?

Kathrine checked the rule book. The section titled "The Marathon" said nothing about the distance being only for men. The entry form said nothing about it either. After all, women weren't supposed to sweat. Women weren't supposed to compete. They were too weak, too fragile, to run that far. That's what most people *still* thought.

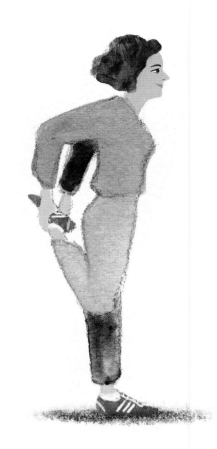

But not Kathrine.

April 19, 1967.

The day of the Boston Marathon.
A record 741 runners registered for the
race, including Kathrine "K. V." Switzer.

The only woman with an official number.

"C'mon runners, let's move on in."

Snow gathered on the race officials' hats as they tried to corral the runners. Kathrine and Arnie jogged around to keep warm before shuffling into the starting area.

The runners moved closer. The crowd fell silent. The gun went off.

BANG!

Away Kathrine ran!

PAT, PAT, PAT, PAT, PAT, PAT, PAT, PAT

The cheers from the crowd were exhilarating. Kathrine smiled.
Faster runners passed by, excited to see a woman in the race.
They wished her well as they continued down the course.
Kathrine relaxed and found her running rhythm.

PAT, PAT, PAT, PAT, PAT, PAT, PAT, PAT
BEEP! BEEP!

"Runners, move to your right!"

A truck filled with newspaper photographers moved through the
pack. A bus carrying race officials followed behind. Runner 261
stood out from the others.

Was that a *girl*?
Wearing a race number?

The photographers wanted pictures.
The race officials wanted her out.

Suddenly, a man stood in the road, blocking Kathrine's way. He reached for her hand and grabbed her glove as she side-stepped past him.

Who *was* that?

SCRIT-SCRIT-

Kathrine heard something behind her. It wasn't like the *pat-pat-pat* of sneakers.

SCRIT-SCRIT-SCRIT-

Kathrine turned to look. A different man, an angrier man, shouted, "Give me those numbers!" He swiped at the front of her shirt.

Kathrine struggled to break free. Arnie tried to push him away.

BOOM!

Another runner barreled into the man and sent him flying off the course. Shaken but freed, Kathrine ran as fast as her legs would take her.

PAT, PAT, PAT, PAT, PAT, PAT, PAT, PAT

For a moment, Kathrine wondered if she should quit. She still had twenty-four miles to go.

Suddenly, finishing wasn't just about her. If she quit now, no one would believe that a woman could run a marathon. People would still say women weren't supposed to sweat. Women weren't supposed to compete. They were too weak, too fragile. They shouldn't be allowed to run.

"No matter what, I have to finish this race," she told Arnie.
"On my hands and knees if I have to."

So Kathrine ran on.

PAT, PAT, PAT, PAT, PAT, PAT, PAT, PAT
12 MILES . . . 14 MILES . . . 16 MILES . . . 18 MILES . . .

Kathrine watched the women standing on the sidelines of the course. Some cheered, but many didn't. If only they knew how magical running was. If only they weren't afraid to try. They could be just like Kathrine. They just didn't know it.

Kathrine rounded the final corner.
Less than two blocks to go . . . just a few more feet . . .
a few steps . . .

26.2 MILES!

Kathrine held her head high and tried to catch her breath.

Reporters surrounded her. "What made you do it?" they asked.
"Why Boston, and why wear numbers?"

Kathrine's answer was simple:

"I like to run.
Women deserve to run too."

Author's Note

Lynchburg Runners
Take on Boston
by K.V. Switzer

It took a lot of hard work, but slowly people started to agree with Kathrine—women deserve to run too. More girls discovered the magic of running. Today, girls everywhere are no longer afraid to try. They no longer stand on the side of the course. They are just like Kathrine: fearless.

It's important to note that Kathrine Switzer did not intentionally mislead race officials. She signed her entry form using her initials, K. V., simply because that's how she was accustomed to signing things (college papers and articles she wrote for the school newspaper). Her health form, which was required for all runners, was completed using her full name. Kathrine even put on makeup and earrings for the race.

Despite the actions of those two Boston Athletic Association officials, Kathrine Switzer completed her historic run of the Boston Marathon in four hours and twenty minutes. Just days after the race, the Amateur Athletic Union expelled Kathrine. Her violations included "running the Boston Marathon with men" and "running the Boston Marathon without a chaperone." But that didn't stop Kathrine from continuing to challenge the all-male dynamic of the distance-running field. She went on to run more than forty marathons. In 1974, seven years after she first ran Boston, Kathrine won the women's division of the New York City Marathon.

In 1978, Kathrine teamed up with Avon® to organize the first Avon® International Women's Marathon. It was the beginning of a successful campaign for the inclusion of the women's marathon event in the Olympic Games in Los Angeles in 1984. For her contributions to the advancement of women's distance running, she was inducted into the National Distance Running Hall of Fame in 1998 and the National Women's Hall of Fame in 2011.